Poetry
Makes me happy
Because I get to tell you how I feel
What's false and what's real
What's in my heart
What rips me apart
The inner parts of my soul
The things I can't control
Life is truly what u make of it
And I'm making sure mine is good like
the cutest outfit
Anyway
Just wanted to say
What was on my mind
Making sure you are a part of my climb
To reach the very top
Ima tell u once again I WILL NEVER
STOP

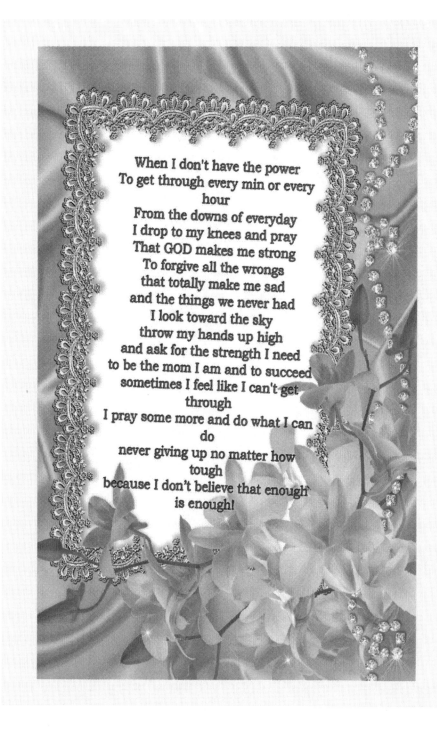

When I don't have the power
To get through every min or every
hour
From the downs of everyday
I drop to my knees and pray
That GOD makes me strong
To forgive all the wrongs
that totally make me sad
and the things we never had
I look toward the sky
throw my hands up high
and ask for the strength I need
to be the mom I am and to succeed
sometimes I feel like I can't get
through
I pray some more and do what I can
do
never giving up no matter how
tough
because I don't believe that enough
is enough!

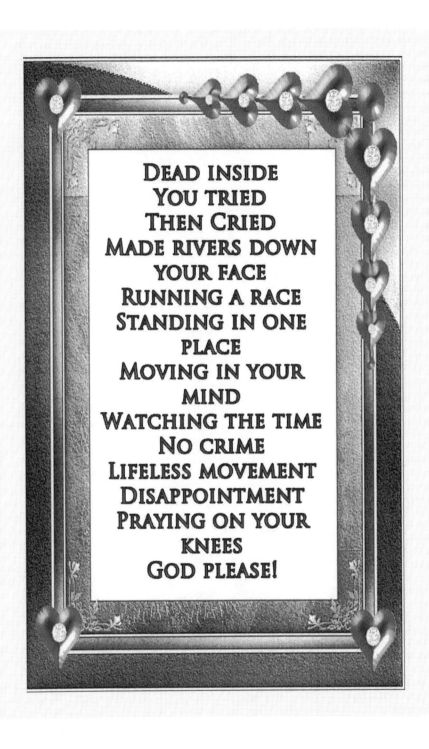

DEAD INSIDE
YOU TRIED
THEN CRIED
MADE RIVERS DOWN
YOUR FACE
RUNNING A RACE
STANDING IN ONE
PLACE
MOVING IN YOUR
MIND
WATCHING THE TIME
NO CRIME
LIFELESS MOVEMENT
DISAPPOINTMENT
PRAYING ON YOUR
KNEES
GOD PLEASE!

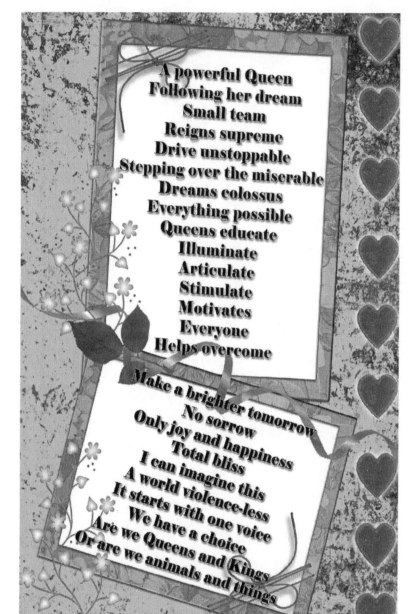

A powerful Queen
Following her dream
Small team
Reigns supreme
Drive unstoppable
Stepping over the miserable
Dreams colossus
Everything possible
Queens educate
Illuminate
Articulate
Stimulate
Motivates
Everyone
Helps overcome

Make a brighter tomorrow
No sorrow
Only joy and happiness
Total bliss
I can imagine this
A world violence-less
It starts with one voice
We have a choice
Are we Queens and Kings
Or are we animals and things

What am I Thankful for
A lot of things I'm sure
But for my children first of all
And for my mother who helped me
stand tall
For each and every blessing bestowed
upon me
For the fact I plan to go down in history
I am Thankful for
So much more
For every person that I can inspire
As I build an inspirational empire
Help people left and right
Doing what I can to give positive insight
I am Thankful for each and every one of
you
And hopeful to help motivate you too!

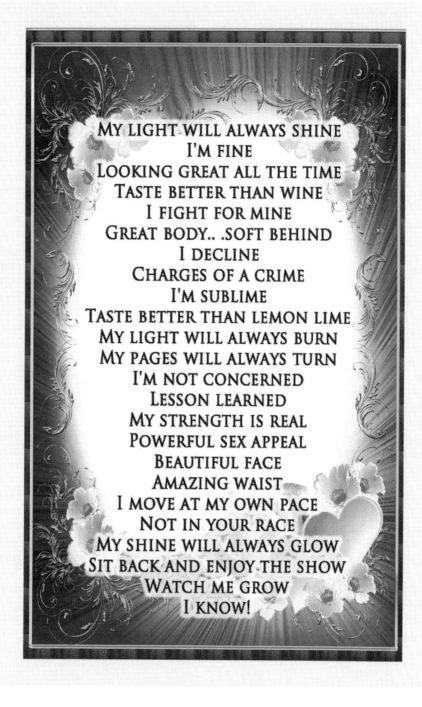

My light will always shine
I'm fine
Looking great all the time
Taste better than wine
I fight for mine
Great body.. .soft behind
I decline
Charges of a crime
I'm sublime
Taste better than lemon lime
My light will always burn
My pages will always turn
I'm not concerned
Lesson learned
My strength is real
Powerful sex appeal
Beautiful face
Amazing waist
I move at my own pace
Not in your race
My shine will always glow
Sit back and enjoy the show
Watch me grow
I know!

Sundays
Lazy ways
Sleepy mode
Freshly washed clothes to fold
Dinner in the oven cooking slow
Gotta feed the kids so they can grow
Getting ready for the work week
Run wild all day on your feet
Sundays the day to fall back
Before the world attacks
So chill with the family
These are the days to make memories
That increase
Our personal peace
Take advantage of the good moments
These are the best events
To recollect in your golden age
So enjoy the tranquil stage
And Sundays are a good place to start

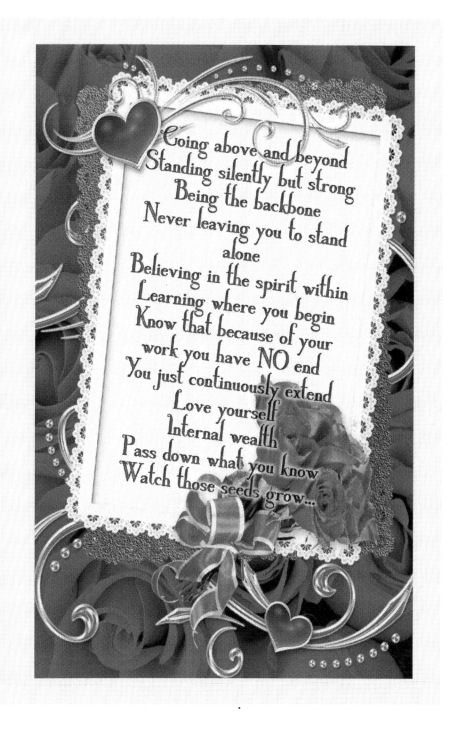

Going above and beyond
Standing silently but strong
Being the backbone
Never leaving you to stand
alone
Believing in the spirit within
Learning where you begin
Know that because of your
work you have NO end
You just continuously extend
Love yourself
Internal wealth
Pass down what you know
Watch those seeds grow...

Love is earned
Yearn
Learn
Be reborn
Adorn
Everything about
you
True
Love
From above

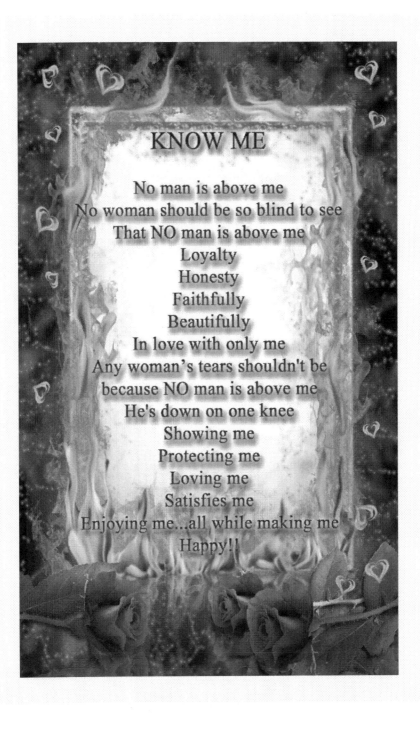

KNOW ME

No man is above me
No woman should be so blind to see
That NO man is above me
Loyalty
Honesty
Faithfully
Beautifully
In love with only me
Any woman's tears shouldn't be
because NO man is above me
He's down on one knee
Showing me
Protecting me
Loving me
Satisfies me
Enjoying me...all while making me
Happy!!

Love

What is Love with no one to give it to
What is caring when it's just you
What is a touch when there so few
What is a team when there not a crew
How can u not be sad
If this was all you had
If you felt like everything was bad
What am I supposed to do when I never
feel glad
That I'm even here on earth
Wondering why my feelings never come
first
Why am I feeling what I feel
Is this even real
I swear it comes and it goes
And I wonder if anybody knows
How I feel deep inside
Does anyone even know why I cried
It's going to be okay
That's what I tell myself everyday

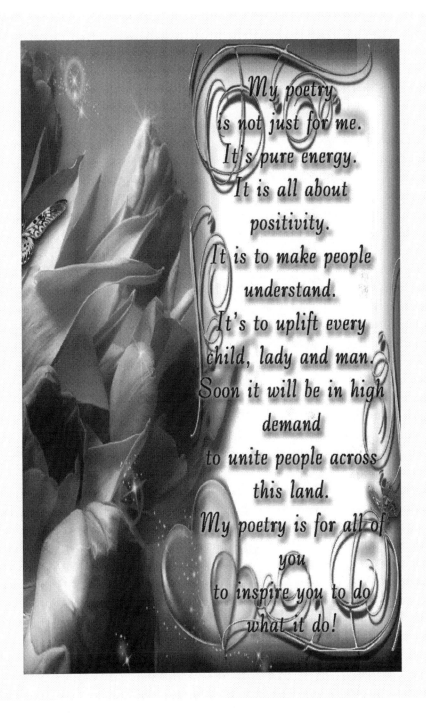

My poetry
is not just for me.
It's pure energy.
It is all about
positivity.
It is to make people
understand.
It's to uplift every
child, lady and man.
Soon it will be in high
demand
to unite people across
this land.
My poetry is for all of
you
to inspire you to do
what it do!

We live in an unjust world
Every person, every boy and
girl
So when you have a family
Hold on cause any one can be
Next.....
So stay blessed
Pray every day
All day
Remember God is love,
It all starts with the one above

Neglect
Regret
No respect
I bet
No dad
Was had
So sad
Mother's tears
Fears
So sincere
Regret
She wept
On her knees
Asked God please
Breathe

What I've learned is
love what you do
There is a destiny
for just you
Love what you are
and you will go far
Shoot for past the
stars
Go for what God has
in store
Love and you will
have more

I ask myself why I go so hard
Why is there only me standing here to
spar
How can I win a fight against myself
Wouldn't that be me fighting for my
health my survival
I'm not a rival
I'm home team
A strong Queen
ready to have this light beam
Time to help these people live a better
dream
That's why I fight nonstop
Making my way to the top
because I know a change gon' come
Making us all look dumb
So I'm educating
While creating
Prepared non-negative souls
That will help this world turn gold
With life, love and laughter
Help stay inspiring ever after.

The Queen needs a King
A promise ring
And not a thing
Will make her disrespect what
God will bring
A real Queen
Will be seen
Where you least expect
She'll be there to protect his
neck
A true King
Can handle anything she will
bring
Kings and Queens know their
worth
They know to each other they
will always come first

What is loyalty
No one seems to show me
Two face fakes
In the grass snakes
Always behind your back
See, loyalty is what people
nowadays lack
Can't be real
Get caught, wanna squeal
What is loyalty…
For me,
Honesty... respectfully true
So hard for most people to do!

Don't look at my thighs
Look into my eyes
Hear my words
Don't look at my curves
This might sound insane
But worry about my brain
Not the soft skin
Worry about the me within
Not what I would feel like
If you held me tight
With all your might
Worry about my mind
Not my soft behind
Spend time not just an hour
My knowledge is my power
Look into my head
No playing games in your bed
I'm a Queen looking for a King

Not scared of anything
That can handle powerful me
Educated incredibly
Working toward greatness
Don't just want to taste this
Don't just look at the flesh
Wanna mesh
Real Kings
Come with rings
Wisdom and brains
Amazing things
Ready to share
Love without fear
Hold you dear
Keep you near
Can see into your eyes
Knowing your power is his prize

Future me
I see
Lights
Bright
Standing ovations
Number one celebrations
High expectations
Motivation
Showing it well
What the hell
I'm moving forward
Toward
Future me
Wait and see

I'm going with life's tugs and pulls
I'm trying to always do right and
follow the rules
I just want to take care of my
children
When I expire, go to heaven
I just make sure I help change a
person
Make them into an inspiring being
To carry on the positive traditions
And pass along all of my creations
As long as they can motivate
And help others to create
And pass this powerful message
That we all must walk our own
Right of Passage
All I'm asking for is peace and love
So that we can walk with the one
above!

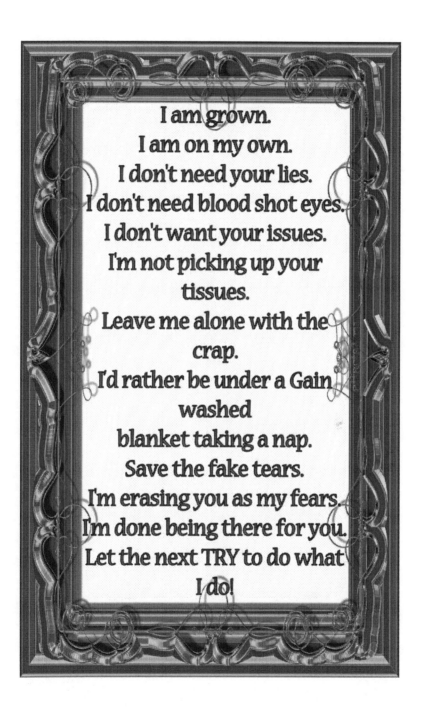

I am grown.
I am on my own.
I don't need your lies.
I don't need blood shot eyes.
I don't want your issues.
I'm not picking up your
tissues.
Leave me alone with the
crap.
I'd rather be under a Gain
washed
blanket taking a nap.
Save the fake tears.
I'm erasing you as my fears.
I'm done being there for you.
Let the next TRY to do what
I do!

Sometimes I feel dead inside
Sometimes I want to run and hide
I'm not the prettiest girl
I've never traveled the world
Sometimes I'm just not sure
What I'm on this earth for
Sometimes I think about not being here
Sometimes I get scared and full of fear
Sometimes I wish GOD would tell me
what to do
Sometimes I wish that I just knew
On those days I don't feel good
As I should
I tell myself
That in sickness and in health
I'm going to love me every day
In every way
Because I deserve to be happy
Even if sometimes I feel crappy
Even if I'm not sexy
I'm always going to be me!

Are you a woman or a mouse?
Are you the head of your house?
Are you a leader?
A superior?
A motivator?
A teacher?
I ask again ladies,
do we not make
and take
Care of the babies?
These kids today don't know nothing.
Not a damn thing.
We are not doing our part.
It all starts
with us women.
We are the beginning and the end.
Girls are running around dropping their
clothes.
Boys going crazy doing only God knows.
Mothers are in the club doing the twerk.
While father's gone cause he's a jerk.
So I'm asking where are the real women
that were sent straight from heaven?

The Rosa Parks' and Maya Angelou's
that know education is the only thing to prove.
Where are my amazing leaders in a dress
that know women are teammates no contest.
Where are the powerful women that work from
their minds?
Not trying to gain from their behinds.
Are you a woman running the show?
Teaching these little ones the right way to grow?
That action speaks louder than words
and lying is so absurd
Teach them right from wrong.
Am asking ladies to please stay strong.
Whether you're alone or with a team,
be the reason these kids beam.
Stop these uneducated, naked crazy folks
that run around killing people for jokes.
Are you a woman strong enough to change the
world?
Strong enough to make men out of boys and
ladies out of girls?
Ladies, Queens and real Women,
it takes you and this is only the beginning!
Women take your place!
Time to win this race!

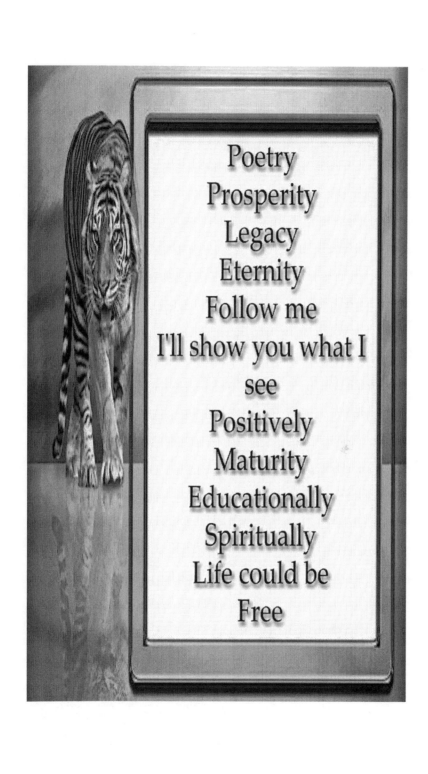

Poetry
Prosperity
Legacy
Eternity
Follow me
I'll show you what I
see
Positively
Maturity
Educationally
Spiritually
Life could be
Free

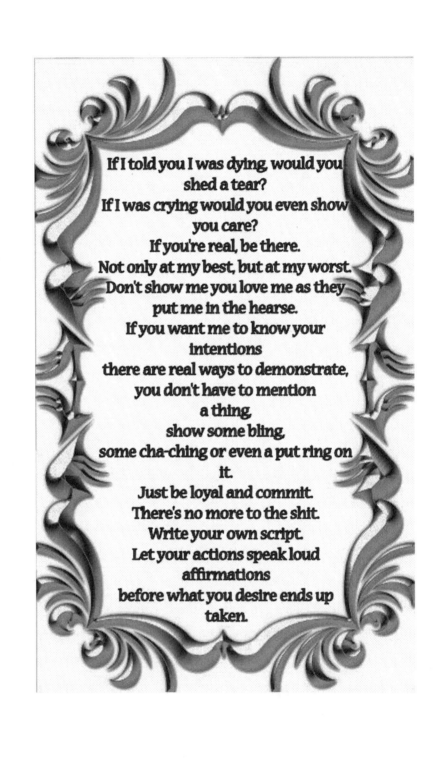

If I told you I was dying, would you
shed a tear?
If I was crying would you even show
you care?
If you're real, be there.
Not only at my best, but at my worst.
Don't show me you love me as they
put me in the hearse.
If you want me to know your
intentions
there are real ways to demonstrate,
you don't have to mention
a thing,
show some bling,
some cha-ching or even a put ring on
it.
Just be loyal and commit.
There's no more to the shit.
Write your own script.
Let your actions speak loud
affirmations
before what you desire ends up
taken.

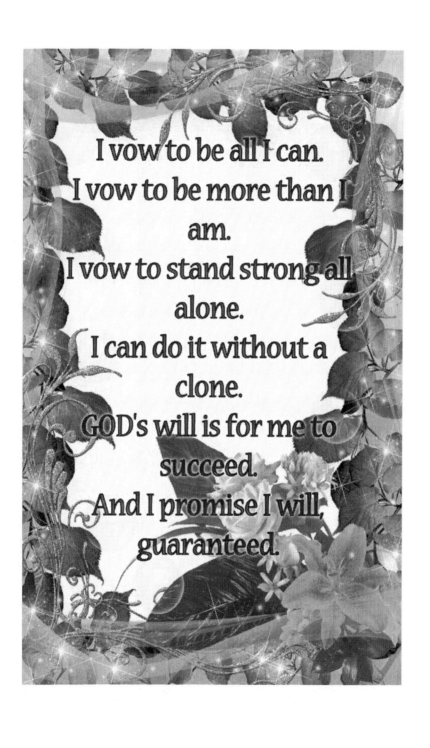

I vow to be all I can.
I vow to be more than I
am.
I vow to stand strong all
alone.
I can do it without a
clone.
GOD's will is for me to
succeed.
And I promise I will,
guaranteed.

Love is thoughtless
Love is a mess
Love is from the heart
Love can tear real love apart
Love is a feeling to your core
No overt thinking you're just secure
Love is your chest heaving
Love is heavy breathing
Love is holding on with every part
of you
Only if that love is really true.

Sometimes in life GOD gives us
signs
He's trying to help us find
The road he wants us to travel
down
With our two feet planted firmly on
the ground
To locate all the good
That would
Not only change the world
But every little boy & girl
So remember always live out your
dreams
No matter how impossible they
seem!

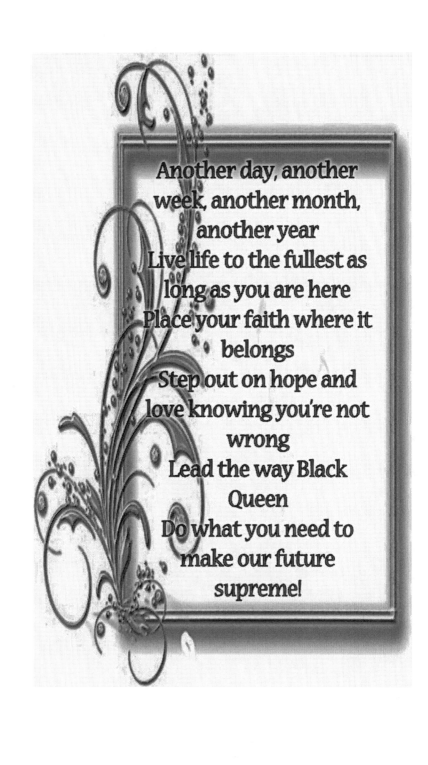

Another day, another week, another month, another year
Live life to the fullest as long as you are here
Place your faith where it belongs
Step out on hope and love knowing you're not wrong
Lead the way Black Queen
Do what you need to make our future supreme!

I'm a woman above all
I was made to be by a man's side not to
crawl
I am strong and free
I express my feelings boisterously
I don't depend on others
Understand not my father or my
mother
The road is mine to travel at the end of
the day
Even if I do it alone I will still pave the
way
For all little girls with a dream
I want them to know you can make it
without a team
Always stand tall and hold your own
Just believe you can do it even standing
alone
Be strong and don't ever fold for no one
Be honest, real and true and you shall
overcome

I sit and stare
Eyes close I still drop a tear
I can stop this pain
Holding it in has me insane
Finally breathing slowly
Demanding control of me
I would like to smile
Be a free as a child
I drop to my knees
To beg and plead
With God to make it better
Instead my face gets wetter
The tears in a race
for a position on my face
I fix myself and stand tall
I'm going to get through it as
true as the writing on the wall.

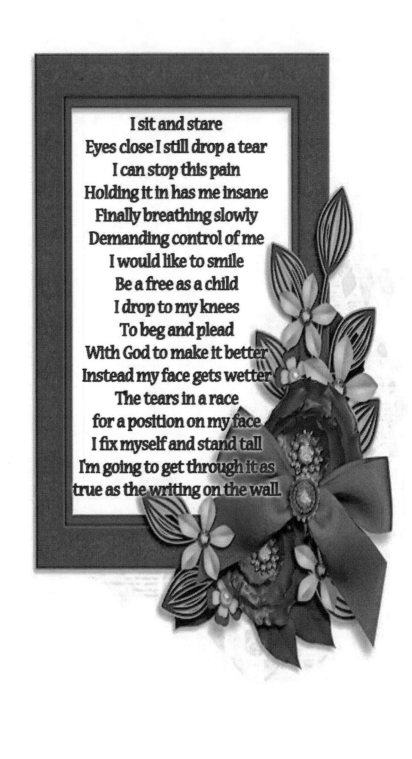

All Lives Matter

Please people, listen to the cries of Ferguson!
This is about LIFE and with ALL of us is where change can begin.
Please stop beating and killing our people.
I'm going to make plain and simple:
Life is valuable no matter the color.
Stop thinking we're different from each other.
Listen to the crying parents all over the planet.
The violence is so senseless.

Love is missing… Love is
being neglected.
This needs to be corrected.
Love each other as God loves
you.
God created us all equal this
is true.
Stop the increase death rate.
Stop the damn hate.
Love each other.
Every man, woman, child,
sister and brother…your
father and mother.
Love is power, love is God.
So spear his children or
receive the rod!

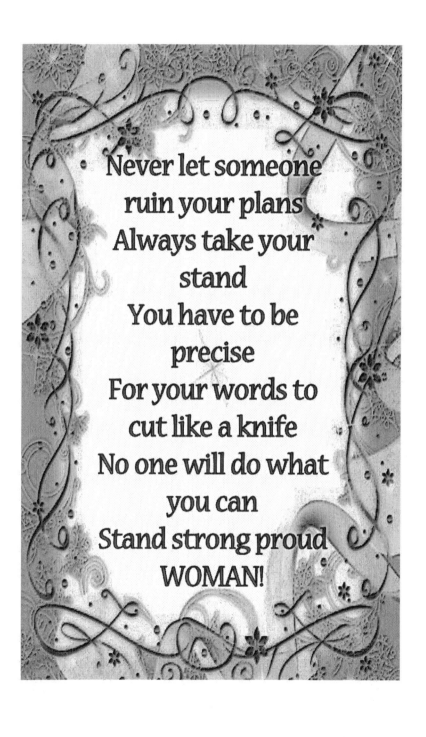

Never let someone
ruin your plans
Always take your
stand
You have to be
precise
For your words to
cut like a knife
No one will do what
you can
Stand strong proud
WOMAN!

Love with all your heart
Love like you'll never
part
Love as hard as you can
Love each and every
man
Love as God loves you
Love because it's the
right thing to do

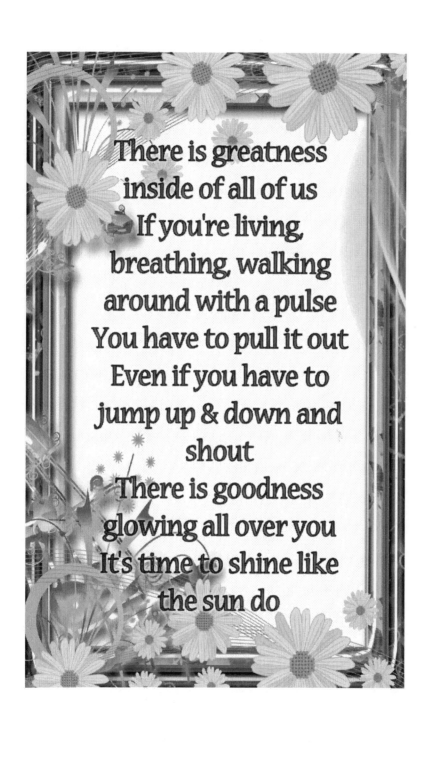

There is greatness
inside of all of us
If you're living,
breathing, walking
around with a pulse
You have to pull it out
Even if you have to
jump up & down and
shout
There is goodness
glowing all over you
It's time to shine like
the sun do

I have been high
I have been low
I believe I can fly
Even without the wind blow
I don't know how to give up
I don't know how to quit
I honestly believe in luck
But I don't know how to just
sit
God is calling me to make a
change
In the next generation
Things can't stay the same
Making moves is my
occupation

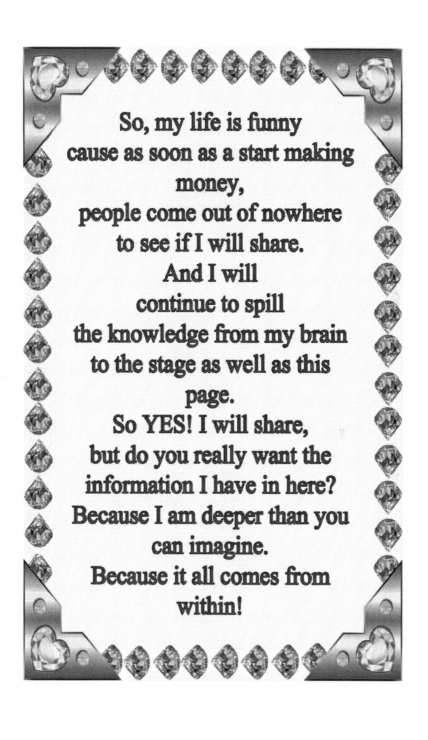

So, my life is funny
cause as soon as a start making
money,
people come out of nowhere
to see if I will share.
And I will
continue to spill
the knowledge from my brain
to the stage as well as this
page.
So YES! I will share,
but do you really want the
information I have in here?
Because I am deeper than you
can imagine.
Because it all comes from
within!

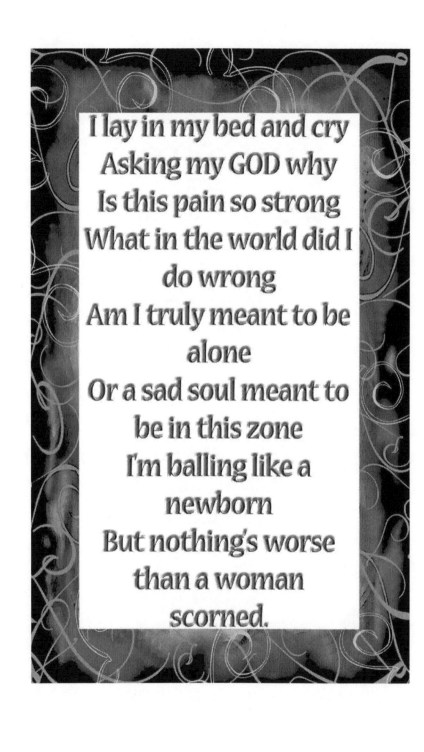

I lay in my bed and cry
Asking my GOD why
Is this pain so strong
What in the world did I
do wrong
Am I truly meant to be
alone
Or a sad soul meant to
be in this zone
I'm balling like a
newborn
But nothing's worse
than a woman
scorned.

Sometime I feel I'm not motivated enough
Making it to the top is so tough
But honestly what's the rush
I mean with all the obstacles and such
It's the journey that makes it worth
Nothing written in stone but death & birth
I'm making it slowly but surely no rush
In the end I'm going to prove how much
Influence personality has on our next
leaders
All our positive leaders and achievers
Keep leading by example keep marching
down that road
No matter how long it takes our stories
must be told.

Happy Father's day
To all the single parents that may
Be doing what they have too
To make ends meet with a few
Dollars...
Trying to be blue collar
Happy Father's day
To everyone is all I wanted to say...

What does it mean
To be a Real Queen
To lead your own team
Guide them through the extreme
Do everything correct nothing to
demean
Never making anyone feel like they're
competing
Knowing together we are
completing
Each other without even seeing
Inside of the next woman's vibe
Just do what you must there's no
being tired
Make power moves with every stride
Walk with you head held high full of
pride.
I am teaching Queens
Explaining exactly what it means
To lead by example

Never tell someone to do
something you cannot do
A Queens golden rule
Treat people the way you want to
be treated and don't be cruel
Each one will teach one how to be
strong
Making sure each one knows
where they belong
Time for all Queens to take their
position
It's time for the journey
No intermissions
Ladies, I hope you're ready for this
big leap
We can only do it together
There's no reason to compete
This is what it means
To be a Real Queen

The claim fame
Wanting people to know your
name
Doing what needs to be done
Never giving up until you're
number 1
Leaving your mark within
others
Helping lonely fathers &
mothers
Giving inspiration where it's
needed
Always winning never
defeating

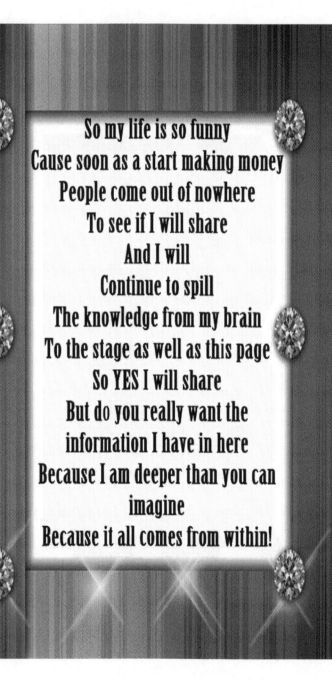

So my life is so funny
Cause soon as a start making money
People come out of nowhere
To see if I will share
And I will
Continue to spill
The knowledge from my brain
To the stage as well as this page
So YES I will share
But do you really want the
information I have in here
Because I am deeper than you can
imagine
Because it all comes from within!

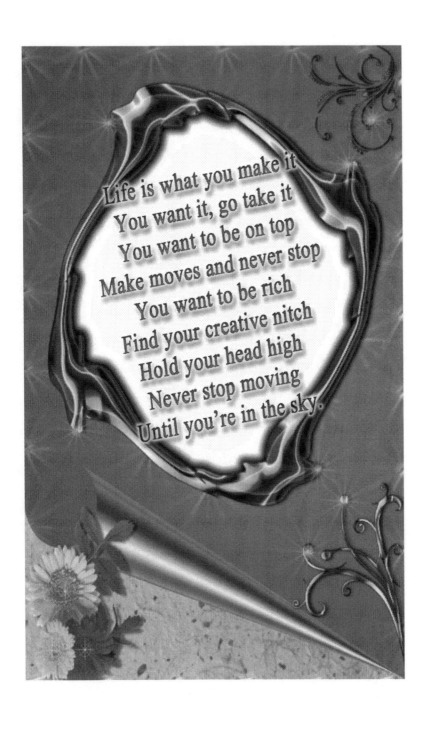

Life is what you make it
You want it, go take it
You want to be on top
Make moves and never stop
You want to be rich
Find your creative nitch
Hold your head high
Never stop moving
Until you're in the sky.

When life gives you
lemons make hot tea
Then you'll see
What keeps you warm or
makes you cold
What's yours to have
and to hold
Make the best of every
situation
There is no room for
hesitation
Run! It's a race to the top
And me personally, I
can't stop!

Single mothers' Friday
drinking away
the week...the day
The pain that over lay
Single mothers' weekend
The bottom of the bottle of Gin
Does it ever end
What a sin
Single mothers drink
Don't think
No spouse
In the house
With the kids all week
Gotta creep
No one to call
Back to the alcohol
A single mothers life
Her sacrifice
Her new dreams

Please HELP us!
Homelessness affects us all.
Whether you're big, short, fat or tall.
This is something we must do our best to fix.
Because we are all at risk
Of losing everything on any day
And would you just want people to walk
away
From you as you ask for a helping hand?
Whether you're a child, woman or man.
So what we need to do is help change this
situation.
Now we are the only ones.
But giving must begin somewhere.
So to be clear.
I am begging for every person to help
whoever and however you can.
This is a personal request not a demand.
We can't make a difference without
everyone.
How would you feel if this was your
daughter or son?
Reach in your pocket and give a penny a
nickel or a dime.

Not to help would be a crime.
We have FAMILIES dying in the street.
Without any food to eat.
And major companies that throw away food
every hour.
Just to show you who has the power.
We as the human race
Need to stand together and face
What's pulling down our Nation.
Life shouldn't be a process of elimination.
We have to stand together pulling up our less
fortunate.
Committed to changing this.....NEVER QUIT!
Until each and every one of us have a place to
call home.
Because the world is a dangerous place to roam.
All alone with nowhere to place to go.
That why we need to show
That all together
We can weather
Any storm that comes our way
The thing is we must help the homeless and that
starts right away!

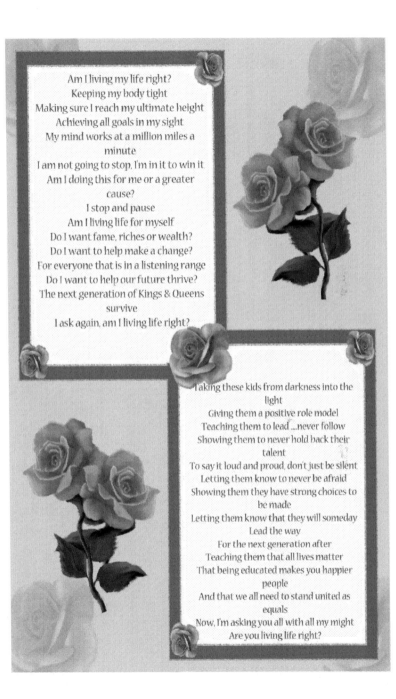

Am I living my life right?
Keeping my body tight
Making sure I reach my ultimate height
Achieving all goals in my sight
My mind works at a million miles a
minute
I am not going to stop, I'm in it to win it
Am I doing this for me or a greater
cause?
I stop and pause
Am I living life for myself
Do I want fame, riches or wealth?
Do I want to help make a change?
For everyone that is in a listening range
Do I want to help our future thrive?
The next generation of Kings & Queens
survive
I ask again, am I living life right?

Taking these kids from darkness into the
light
Giving them a positive role model
Teaching them to lead ...never follow
Showing them to never hold back their
talent
To say it loud and proud, don't just be silent
Letting them know to never be afraid
Showing them they have strong choices to
be made
Letting them know that they will someday
Lead the way
For the next generation after
Teaching them that all lives matter
That being educated makes you happier
people
And that we all need to stand united as
equals
Now, I'm asking you all with all my might
Are you living life right?

In times of need
People show you who they really are
indeed
they turn their back in a hurry
Act like mice and scurry
Act like roaches when you turn the
lights on
turn around and they're all gone
Untouchable... invisible not there
they disappeared into thin air
So lean on you
Do what you gotta do
trust those that show you the
deserve it
The ones that got your back when
shit gets thick
The one that might be down but
never out
even in a drought
they're a dying breed
So if you know one take heed
but still learn to depend on you
And always do what you got to!

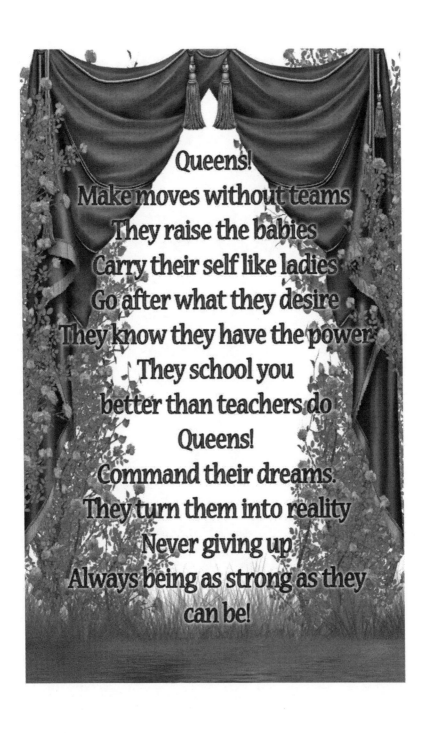

Queens!
Make moves without teams
They raise the babies
Carry their self like ladies
Go after what they desire
They know they have the power
They school you
better than teachers do
Queens!
Command their dreams.
They turn them into reality
Never giving up
Always being as strong as they
can be!

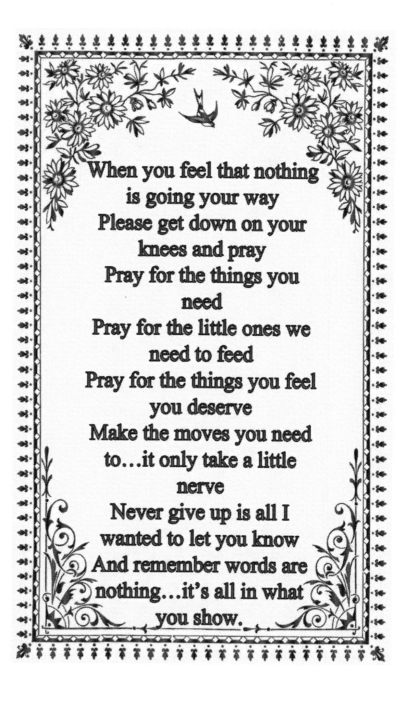

When you feel that nothing
is going your way
Please get down on your
knees and pray
Pray for the things you
need
Pray for the little ones we
need to feed
Pray for the things you feel
you deserve
Make the moves you need
to…it only take a little
nerve
Never give up is all I
wanted to let you know
And remember words are
nothing…it's all in what
you show.

I don't understand what I did wrong
Why I'm always crying to one sad love
song
All I want is to touched by someone
who really loves me
Someone who can see
the pain I've lived and survived
The reason every day I rise
I give my heart and soul
Only to be left in the cold
I want people to stop looking at my
walk
And understand the words I talk
I need people to read my eyes
And not worry about what's between
my thighs
I'm sick of being hurt
Sick of people doing me dirt
I am a Queen
On my own damn team
I need real love
One that's unconditional and can only
be given from above!

I sit back enraged
Watching these young kids engage
It's violent
With malicious intent
The young girls are worse than the boys
The worst part is you can see these action bring them joy
I sit here enraged
Wondering why these kids act like they should be in a cage
I put my pen to pad
To explain how bad
To express just how mad
No no no... How sad...
This makes a mother of four...
I'm scared for them to walk out the door
People ain't living right
Police killing everything in sight
Everybody wants to fight
I wanna hold them tight

Keep them safe from all the pain
The world is going insane
Please hear me y'all
Stand proud and tall
If your child trips... Let 'em fall
Then pick them up, brush them off, hug them that's all
If you hear about child neglect or abuse
Report it!!! These kids need us and that's the truth
Help when and where you can
Amen Amen
I sit here and think about my children
I think...Save them all. God.. Amen...
Help us all stop the violence
Uphold the benevolence
Pure are the lives that haven't lived yet
Protect

Purity
Maturity
Knowledge
Let it live..
No longer enraged
My pen has engaged
Please help build
All the boys and girls
Send them in a positive direction
Teach them and give them love and affection
Stop watching these kids fight
Let's teach them what's right
Get them out the street, give them something to do
Shit! Parents keep them with you
Just please be aware
Don't just sit there!!!

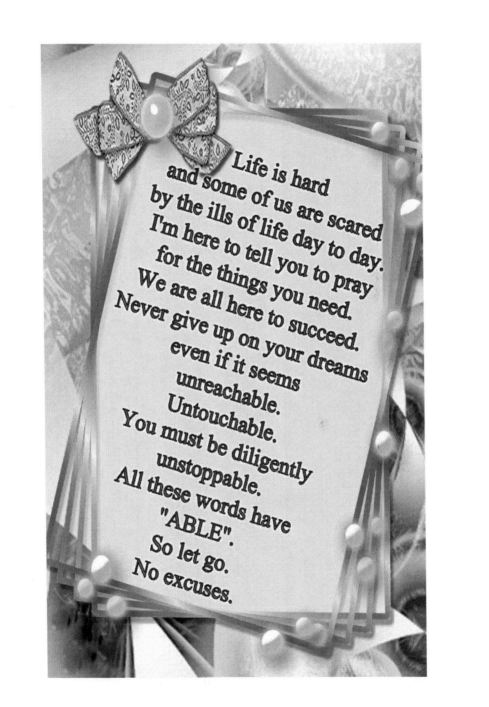

Life is hard
and some of us are scared
by the ills of life day to day.
I'm here to tell you to pray
for the things you need.
We are all here to succeed.
Never give up on your dreams
even if it seems
unreachable.
Untouchable.
You must be diligently
unstoppable.
All these words have
"ABLE".
So let go.
No excuses.

Make the best of what you
have…NO refuses
Don't let nothing or no one
hold you back.
If they don't believe in
you…they're whack.
So charge forward with all
your might.
Keep your dreams in sight
and take flight…
I'll see you there
cause remember just like
GOD…I'm everywhere.

When you're in love so deep
When they're sad, you weep.
When they're shy, you try
And you try
With all of you
To pull them through.
Lift them back up at any cost.
Anybody in the way they're getting
tossed.
You love so hard.
There is no regard
For anything...
It's all about your boo thing.
You breathe them, inhale them.
Wanna surround yourself in them.
Love that strong has to have
communication.
Can't get love in all that infatuation.
Love right and from the your core.
Intermingled minds love harder,
more mature.
Feel the love down in your soul
Then you can give the love all the
way down to your toes.

The snow is falling so fast
Life is just going past
Things moving at a quick pace
We're getting better as a human race
The days are getting shorter
So take care of your sons and daughters
Before you know it your kids will be grown
And out in this on their own
So teach them right from wrong
Because it won't be long
Until they're all alone
Calling you on the phone
Telling their life story
As a parent I know we worry
But know just as the snow is pure
Our children will mature
And make moves toward a better tomorrow
And your lead is what they follow
So make it clear as the rain
That nothing has to stay the same
Make it as bright
As the sun's light
Make it as pure as the falling snow
That eventually we all have to positively
grow
And there is always someone looking up to
us
So doing the best you can is a must!

BREATHE... Take the air all the way to your chest
Close your eyes and release that breath
Take yourself inside your own mind
Leave all your turmoil behind
Search your soul for purpose and reason
Know you are a defining force NOT just a season
Build up the courage, the strength, the power
Because with each passing hour
That you wait
Hesitate
You miss out on the favor
That our savior
Has in store for your spirit
It's up to you to feel it
Breathe
Take the air to your chest
Know that you are the best
You can overcome
Do not succumb
No more waiting
Hesitating
Feel your world inflating
So work toward your purpose
The past was bad no need to repeat it
Move straight forward
Toward

The thought GOD designed you for
Push through the door
Don't wait for opportunity
Build your own community
There is a reason we are all here
You can figure it out or just sit there
Me....Personally 1- Breathe
Then I take the air to my chest
Knowing I cannot rest
Feeling I must help insight change
Thought = deranged
That is my purpose and reason
I am a defining force NOT just a season
All it takes is the courage to believe
The strength to just breathe
Knowing what we have to achieve
To ensure our future will be a relief
I will never succumb
I know we have the power to overcome
It's not going to happen in all one breath
It's going to take time...but I'm here till death

I want to say this loud and clear
I am a proud Queen with nothing to fear.
Yes, I might have four children,
However nothing about them is a sin.
I was never a slut, a hoe or a whore
And I am very proud of everything I had to
endure.
Though out of wedlock I bared four children
They came from my own decision.
I could have had an abortion
But living life, come procreation.
I love all my babies all the same.
This is my life, not a game.
I am strong.
I work hard and long
To give them everything I never had.
Even if I am not with any of their dads
They will always know that mommy is here
And because of me they have nothing to fear.
I am a Queen.
They are my team.
From them my light will always beam
And my power will always stream
Through my children.
They are my greatest extension.
The relationships with their fathers were years
more than four
However, no amount of time can keep someone
from walking out the front door.
But my mind is mature

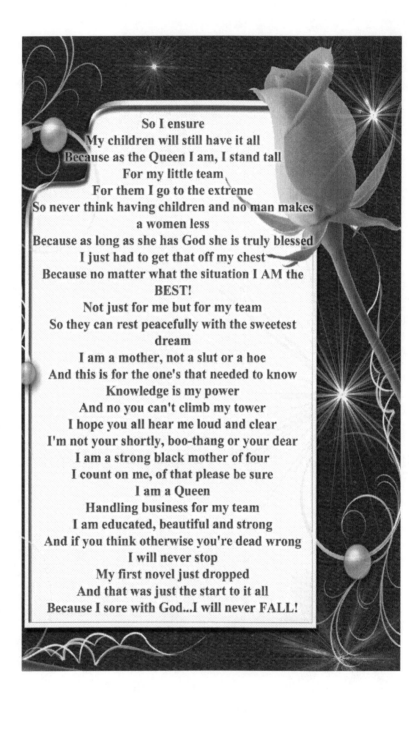

So I ensure
My children will still have it all
Because as the Queen I am, I stand tall
For my little team
For them I go to the extreme
So never think having children and no man makes
a women less
Because as long as she has God she is truly blessed
I just had to get that off my chest
Because no matter what the situation I AM the
BEST!
Not just for me but for my team
So they can rest peacefully with the sweetest
dream
I am a mother, not a slut or a hoe
And this is for the one's that needed to know
Knowledge is my power
And no you can't climb my tower
I hope you all hear me loud and clear
I'm not your shortly, boo-thang or your dear
I am a strong black mother of four
I count on me, of that please be sure
I am a Queen
Handling business for my team
I am educated, beautiful and strong
And if you think otherwise you're dead wrong
I will never stop
My first novel just dropped
And that was just the start to it all
Because I sore with God...I will never FALL!

Sometimes I cry
Sometimes I ask God, Why?
Sometimes I wonder why me
Sometimes I'm sadder than
anyone can see
I cry tears of pain
Tears of hurt all the same
I smile behind it because I have
to
I push hard straight through
On the inside
Knowing I've died
Mental...physical...emotional
Loosen all control

Asking God why does not one
person have my back
What in my mental isn't
straight from all those
attacks
I feel like something is
holding me down
There is no one around
Sometimes I ask myself why
Why am I shy?
What is pride?
Should I let mine take over or
enjoy the ride?
Because sometimes I cry
I also laugh...and giggle and
smile
Then I hear God ... It's coming,
It's just going to take a while...

I just had to leave a poem tonight
Drop a little of my insight
Let you people know everything's
alright
Let your know I'm still marching for
our cause
Let you know there is never any
pause
Poetry speaks loud and clear
Even when it's silently just sitting
there
I'm meeting goals everyday
Striving to be greater in every way
Doing what has to be done for my
survival
The things I that will make me
unbreakable
Building a stronger generation
Where spoken word has an endless
collection
With a strong positive impact
Because I, Queen Amina will never
give up and that's a fact!

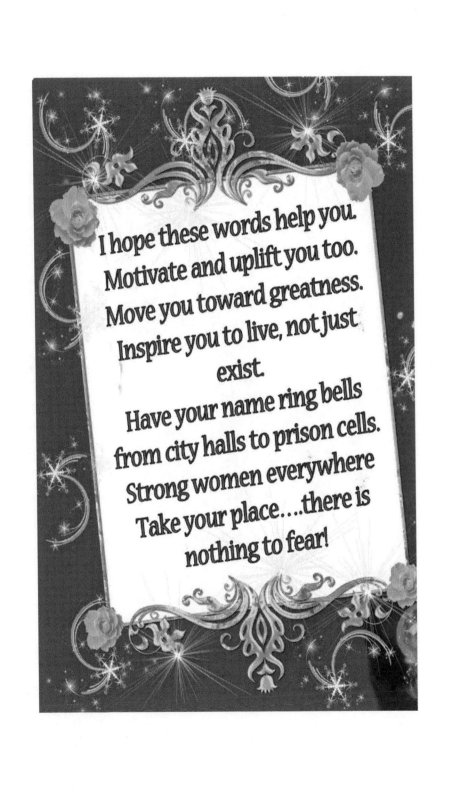

I hope these words help you.
Motivate and uplift you too.
Move you toward greatness.
Inspire you to live, not just exist.
Have your name ring bells from city halls to prison cells.
Strong women everywhere
Take your place....there is nothing to fear!

Thank you
For all you do
Thank you
For always being true
Thank you very much
For being real enough to touch
Thank you from my heart
I promise we shall never part
At the end of the day
I just want to say
Thank you
To everyone who
Believed in my journey
And honestly wish well upon me!

ENTER THE MIND OF THE QUEEN

ENTER THE MIND OF THE QUEEN

Made in the USA
Middletown, DE
11 April 2021

37409063R00050